**CD INCLUDES
15 FULL-BAND TRACKS**

west coast jazz piano

An In-Depth Look at the Styles of the Masters
by Gene Rizzo

Cover photos:

Billy Childs by John Clayton/Windham Hill Records

Vince Guaraldi courtesy of Fantasy, Inc.

Dave Brubeck by William "PoPsie" Randolph

Russ Freeman from Retna

André Previn from Photofest

ISBN 978-1-4234-1912-9

**Hal • LEONARD®
CORPORATION**

7777 W. BLUEMOUND RD. P.O. BOX 13819 MILWAUKEE, WI 53213

In Australia Contact:
Hal Leonard Australia Pty. Ltd.
4 Lentara Court
Cheltenham, Victoria, 3192 Australia
Email: ausadmin@halleonard.com.au

Visit Hal Leonard Online at
www.halleonard.com

INTRODUCTION

East Coast versus West Coast jazz was the mother of all jazz schisms in the 1950s. The conventional wisdom was that East Coasters blew hot and West Coasters blew cool. In spite of numerous exceptions to the rule, the debate raged on for a decade. It all became a moot point with the British rocker invasion of the 1960s and the rash of folk singers who followed. They claimed squatters' rights in the clubs and on college campuses while jazz went underground to lick its wounds.

Jazz has since surfaced stronger than ever before, but vestiges of the old seaboard wars still linger. This book hopes to make the case that the West Coast has produced at least as many hard swinging musicians as its Eastern counterpart, and particularly on piano.

All tunes in this book are original works composed in the styles of the featured artists. The accompanying CD features both full band and play-along tracks of each tune.

DEDICATION

This one is for my dear uncle, Anthony J. Ritts; humorist, sketch artist, and composer of church music.

CONTENTS

Photo courtesy of Photofest, Inc.

DAVE BRUBECK
(1920–)

BIOGRAPHY

Concord, California is no longer the fertile ranching and farming community it was when David Warren Brubeck was born. Decades later, the newly built Concord Pavilion, surrounded by office parks, residential neighborhoods, and fast food franchises, would host the celebrated Brubeck quartet. More than 10,000 people were in attendance on land that Brubeck's father once oversaw as a cattle-ranch manager. The family's matriarch was a classical pianist who gave her son music lessons, patiently allowing for sight-reading problems due to his poor vision. Her pupil began his professional career at age 13. In 1938, Brubeck flirted briefly with zoology at the College of the Pacific. Switching his major to music, and composition in particular, he enrolled in Darius Milhaud's class at Mills College. While serving in the armed forces in WWII, Brubeck took a few contentious lessons with Arnold Schoenberg before teacher and pupil mutually decided to part company.

The pianist's immediate post-war career was marked by restless experiments with instrumentation. An octet reflecting Milhaud's heady principles of polytonality and counterpoint proved to be as unmarketable as a sommelier at a sports bar. But a trio with a bassist and Cal Tjader doubling on vibes and drums yielded a cult following, devoted enough to encourage another group configuration. In the summer of 1951, Brubeck added alto saxophonist Paul Desmond to a conventional rhythm section and struck gold. The unit freely indulged in counterpoint, polytonality, and unconventional time signatures to surprising commercial success, even as critics and musicians debunked the music for "not swinging" and "questionable jazz credentials."

Before the quartet disbanded in 1967, it recorded the first million-selling LP in jazz history (*Time Out*, 1960), and sustained an enviable history of playing to SRO audiences worldwide. Brubeck has since led other groups (occasionally appearing with his sons Chris, Danny, and Darius), but devotes the lion's share of his time to composing large-scale oratorios such as *The Light in the Wilderness*.

ANALYSIS: *Body Heat*

Except for the free application of counterpoint and Paul Desmond's meadowlark sound on alto, the Brubeck quartet's ties to West Coast jazz are tenuous at best. Even the leader's often ham-fisted playing was "hotter" than the approach of pianists in Los Angeles, where cooler heads prevailed. Overall, Brubeck comes under the West Coast jazz rubric more geographically than musically.

Since the release of *Time Out* and the follow-up session *Time Further Out*, Brubeck has been misperceived as a wholesaler of oddball meters. The fact is, his best-known compositions (i.e., "The Duke" and "In Your Own Sweet Way"), and arguably his most creative playing, are cast in common time. "Body Heat" explores a vintage period for Brubeck as a soloist—the 1950s—when he built his improvisations exclusively on the bedrock of songs by great American composers.

The first sixteen bars of the example look like hymnal notation. The absence of syncopation and the predominance of block chords in unison rhythm suggest a sturdy Lutheran chorale, not a jazz solo. Sections like this, frequent in the Brubeck canon, invite his severest critics to dismiss him for not swinging. A closer look at letter A, however, reveals other redeeming virtues. The harmony, nearly always a preoccupation with Brubeck, is an effective mix of voicing procedures: *root position* (the chord fundamental/root is the lowest note), *inversion* (the root appears in a higher part of the chord), *drop-two voicing* (the second voice below the lead of an inverted four-part chord is dropped an octave), and *doubled lead* (the lead is replicated at a lower octave). Although drop-two does most of the heavy lifting here, the interchange with the other procedures is not as obvious as it could be because of careful voice leading. The chordal movement is drawn from familiar jazz syntax: bar 15 contains ii–V sequences that would make any bebopper proud. Even when Brubeck shuns jazz traditions of rhythm, his harmony is rarely less than the genuine article.

Section B is more lyrical. The upward spiraling quarter-note triplets pause briefly at bar 20 quoting "All God's Chillun' Got Rhythm." Brubeck is fond of such interpolations. Were there a category in the *Guinness Book of World Records* for "Most Songs Quoted in a Jazz Career," either Brubeck or his alter ego, Paul Desmond, would handily win it. The quarter-note triplet motif resumes at bar 21. It can logically do so because it answers in D minor the previous four bars, which were grounded in D major.

We find syncopation for the first time at bar 24. It continues with a freer, post-Bud Powell use of the left hand in section C. Apparently, Brubeck is acquainted with the jazz mainstream (before the current broad definition of the music), but chooses not to be limited by it. Two of the pianist's melodic hallmarks appear here: the prominent use of 13ths (bar 26) and repeated top notes over shifting harmony (bars 31 and 32).

The channel (or bridge) comes 'round again at letter D. Couched in 18th century counterpoint, this is the kind of Brubeck that hardcore jazz fans once found particularly off-putting. No blues inflections or groove-oriented riffing corrupt this courtly two-part invention. Bars 33–36 are rendered in strict imitation. Bars 37–40 spin out in free counterpoint. Both lines are mutually independent in the manner of Bach and Handel. To his credit, Brubeck can improvise such knotty things with amazing ease.

A rhythmic configuration (two sixteenth notes followed by an eighth note) which first appears in bar 9 is recalled in bar 41. It spearheads a dense chordal sequence, and after a pair of bare 5ths, does it again (bars 43 and 44). More two-part counterpoint lightens the texture at bar 45. Repeated top notes are perched on the final, widely-voiced chords.

Body Heat

Music by Gene Rizzo

Photo by Nathaniel Welch

BILLY CHILDS
(1957–)

BIOGRAPHY

Right out of the gate of his career, pianist/composer Billy Childs was keeping the company of heavy hitters. Even before graduating from the University of Southern California with a degree in composition, the native Californian joined J.J. Johnson and Nat Adderley for a gig in Japan. The six years with Freddie Hubbard which followed—and other stints with Eddie Daniels, Bobby Hutcherson, and Branford Marsalis—added a solid grounding in jazz tradition to a pre-existing classical technique. A savvy accompanist, Childs has appeared intermittently with vocalist Diane Reeves since 1979.

His Los Angeles-based quartet, formed in the 1980s, reflected his growing dedication to the spiritual values in the music of John Coltrane. Among the quartet's members, tenor sax player Bob Sheppard has made valuable contributions to a string of the leader's recordings for Windham Hill Jazz, beginning in 1988 with *Take This for Example*. Later releases showcased Childs's expertise with electric keyboards and other gadgetry.

Childs's playing is influenced by post-moderns like Herbie Hancock, McCoy Tyner, and Chick Corea. The ghosts of his writing models—Duke Ellington, Paul Hindemith, and William Walton—haunt his *Concerto for Piano and Jazz Chamber Orchestra*. The work was premiered at the Monterey Jazz Festival in 1995.

For a musician whose extensive travels and exposure to many musical cultures have made him a World Music advocate, Childs's eclecticism is admirably diverse without being scattershot. He is currently exploring his resourceful imagination in the touring band of Chris Botti.

ANALYSIS: *Prince of the City*

About the frequent use of mixed meter in his compositions, Childs writes, "The reason is because that's how I hear it—I hear asymmetrically." Jazz players have been seduced by irregular bar-line divisions since Dave Brubeck's *Time Out* album (1959) made them popular. Experimental outpourings as clumsy as a one-legged sack race were rampant. What makes Childs the exception rather than the rule as a composer is the fluid inevitability of his creations. His "blowing" sections, however, are usually framed in conventional time, and it is Childs the soloist, after all, who concerns us here.

"Prince of the City" is content to sustain a uniform signature throughout, the better to demonstrate Childs's more accessible ideas about melody, harmony, and rhythm. After the intro establishes key (D minor) and tempo, the piece settles into a minor blues "head" with the traditional 12-bar count doubled to 24. The Dorian mode (D to D in the C major scale) informs most of the head starting on D (bars 17–24), is transposed to G Dorian (bars 25–28), and returns to D (bars 29–32). Non-tertian chords (in this case chords based on fourths rather than thirds), heard almost exclusively at letter A, are a Childs staple. Like many postmoderns, he is attracted to their "floating" quality. The old major-minor system cuts in at bar 33, approaching a cadence with a prickly voiced V chord (bars 34–35). Modality is reclaimed before the repeat sign.

Those acquainted with Childs's Windham Hill recordings will find echoes of them in much of "Prince of the City," such as the treble-clef chords with fourths enclosed in bare fifths in section B. Chords and single notes jointly stress the D fundamental of the key from bars 41–48. Notably, the temporary modulation to G minor beginning at bar 48 is effected without a D7 secondary dominant, thereby retaining modal integrity. The chords in bars 57–60 generate two lines; one ascending and the other descending. All of this represents Childs in high gear, driving with the kind of intensity he generally brings to fast tempos.

The second chorus, section C, introduces a volatile rhythmic figure for the left hand. Marking the first and last beat in each bar of its recurrence, the figure accompanies the right hand with insistent perfect 5ths. The modulation to G minor (bar 72) sidesteps a secondary dominant again (see bar 48) by way of a semitonal exchange in the melody line on beats 3 and the "and" of 4: B is the 6th degree of D Dorian, and moves to C, the 11th of G minor, without incident. Childs also references some Bill Evans-type voicings (bars 73–77) before laying out the richest sounding chord in the entire piece, the G13 augmented 11 in bars 79–80. *Pentatonics* (melodic ideas based on five-note scales with no fourths or sevenths) take on the dominant chords of bars 81–84, and the chorus ends modally.

The coda is a joyful rhythm jam, suggested by the concluding bars of the last chorus. Basically, the harmonic scheme is a repeated two-bar vamp in the D Phyrigian mode (D–E♭–F–G–A–B♭–C–D). The top voices shift from chord root to fifth to help prevent the paired sequence from wearing out its welcome. Childs has a brief encounter with a traditional tonality V chord in the final bars, but concludes on a Phyrigian cadence.

Prince of the City

TRACK 3
Full Band

TRACK 4
Rhythm Track

Music by Gene Rizzo

Bright Samba ♩ = 220
Play 4 times (drums, 3rd & 4th time)

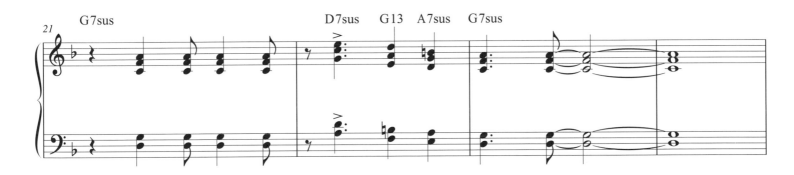

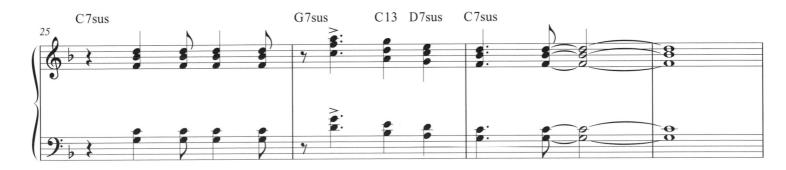

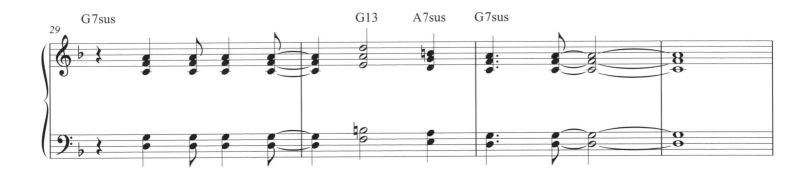

Photo by The Institute of Jazz Studies

VIC FELDMAN
(1934–1987)

BIOGRAPHY

From the 1940s through the mid-1950s, a small group of British jazz players crossed the Big Pond to play their art in the USA. Barely enough people to fill a bus stop kiosk, their collective impact on jazz was unexpectedly huge. The careers of George Shearing, Marian McPartland, and Leonard Feather serve to suggest the extent of that impact. Among the most gifted, if lesser known of the emigrants, is the former child actor and multi-instrumentalist (drums, vibes, and piano) Vic Feldman.

Feldman's reputation as a triple threat preceded him when he settled in Los Angeles in 1955. Once a side-man with such boldface-name Brits as Ted Heath, Ronnie Scott, and Ralph Sharon, his first eager state-side employers were Woody Herman and Buddy DeFranco. In 1957, he joined the Lighthouse All Stars, a standard-issue West Coast Jazz unit, where he was featured mostly on vibes. Feldman's career as a pianist took a surprising turn in 1959 when he subbed for Russ Freeman on Shelly Manne's superb four-volume set of live recordings from San Francisco's Blackhawk club. Manne's recent conversion to hard bop at the time brought out the best in Feldman. His clean, fleet pianistics set the bar high for most vibes/piano doublers, a breed usually limited to a two-fingered keyboard technique.

Cannonball Adderley hired Feldman on the strength of the Blackhawk recordings. Touring with Adderley (1960–61) marks his only national exposure as a featured artist. In 1963, Miles Davis tried to lure Feldman away from Los Angeles after they recorded some exquisite ballad performances for an album that borrows its title from the pianist's original composition *Seven Steps to Heaven*. But he was fielding a barrage of calls for film, TV, and studio work, and chose to remain homebound. Feldman eventually became one of the premier session men in Southern California. Before his untimely death, he had worked on projects as diverse as the soundtrack for *The Sandpiper*, and albums with Joni Mitchell and Steely Dan.

ANALYSIS: *Timeline*

Drummer Shelly Manne fronted the most exciting small group of his career in 1959. Previously associated with formal experiments, heavily arranged frameworks, and other trappings of West Coast Jazz since settling in California in 1952, the ex-New Yorker recorded his new free-wheeling quintet live in the crown jewel night spot of the Bay area, the Blackhawk. Vic Feldman provided damage control accompaniment for the band when needed, in addition to fine solos.

"Timeline" is based on the cogent musicality the pianist exhibited on the Blackhawk sessions. The intro's major 7th chords are in the second inversion whereby their fundamentals (or roots) grind semitonally against the 7ths. Feldman tweaks his harmony like this whenever possible. A persistent left-hand ostinato identifies the key of G major regardless of the several notes foreign to the scale heard in the chords.

Section A juxtaposes eight languorous bars with eight bars of restless activity. Bars 13–20 unfold in lush five-part voicings with the lead doubled an octave below. Bars 21–28 discard the ostinato, and booted along by the shift from a Latin to a swing groove, two unresolved 11th chords try to escape the scale's tyranny (bars 24–26). Coming up on letter B (bars 27–29), a V–I sequence reclaims the key center with typically Feldmanesque alterations of the harmony. Dominant 7th chords are easy targets for adventurous harmonists because of their volatility.

At bar 39, we come to the final section of "Timeline's" A-B-A-C form in which a II–V exchange (B to E chords in bars 39–40) precedes an A13 with a subtle modification: its 5th is flatted. The pianist cannot resist the opportunity to dust the voicing with a pinch of pepper. The V chord just before the solo break is also "seasoned" (the flat 5 and flat 9 of the D7alt chord).

The one-handed line through section C makes expressive use of a wider range compass than is generally preferred by other pianists. If the appreciable interval gaps in the line seem more two-mallet friendly (vibistic?) than five-finger friendly, we shouldn't be surprised in Feldman's case (also see bars 89–90). In bars 53–60 the left hand enhances the graceful line in the right: the flurry of sixteenth notes (bars 53–54) briefly implies double time. The longest held note in Section D (bars 73–74) occasions some active left-hand work for contrast. We reach a convincing V–I cadence in spite of the unresolved voicing of the dominant chord.

Feldman's playing at the Blackhawk is rife with the procedure heard at letter E: a densely chorded, rhythmic figure sets up a spate of single-noted passages somewhat in the way good big band ensemble writing introduces a soloist. (Note how the "soloist" frames his phrases in rhyming couplets.) There are two exchanges of this practice before the D.S. The coda is a tranquilized variation of the intro.

Although not an immediately recognizable stylist, Feldman was a powerhouse swinger with an unerring sense of symmetry. How he achieved that symmetry while freely utilizing varied materials warrants close scrutiny.

Timeline

TRACK 5
Full Band

TRACK 6
Rhythm Track

Music by Gene Rizzo

Latin ♩ = 160
Play 3 times (treble 2nd & 3rd time)

Photo © Retna

RUSS FREEMAN
(1926–2002)

BIOGRAPHY

Russ Freeman, the cousin of composer/lyricist Ray Gilbert and singer Joanne Gilbert, was born in Chicago and raised in Los Angeles. His four years of classical piano study ended at age 12. One of the first West Coast pianists to embrace bebop (via faithful attendance at Billy Berg's Vine Street Club during Charlie Parker and Dizzy Gillespie's historic gig of 1945), he joined Howard McGhee's group in 1947, which Parker virtually co-led. Rising from a regional phenomenon to a bi-coastal luminary while serving as pianist, musical director, and road manager for the Chet Baker quartet (1953), Freeman's opportunity to expose his considerable talent to a wider audience came at a price—Baker, a hopeless drug addict, was a box of snakes off the bandstand. An association between two otherwise perfectly synergized artists ended amicably in 1957, and Baker would never again sustain such a consistent level of creativity.

When not touring with Benny Goodman (1955–59)—who curiously limited his pianists' comping to the upper half of the instrument—Freeman was in completely felicitous company with Shelly Manne (1956–57). Manne recorded the pianist's composition "The Wind," about which more will follow. Several fruitful collaborations between Freeman and Art Pepper were recorded in the late 1950s.

From the 1960s on, the pianist's resume shows an active commercial work history (e.g., Musical Director for Mitzi Gaynor, among other surprising employers). Gradually, he lost footing in the jazz community. Occasional reunions with Art Pepper and Shelly Manne in the recording studio never reclaimed his former glory. Freeman's fetching ballad, "The Wind," became a cash cow when Mariah Carey included it on her hit album *Emotions* (1991). His part of the take provided a new home in Las Vegas and a comfortable retirement.

ANALYSIS:
A Clumsy Girl Named Grace

In the 1950s, Freeman hammered out a style that set him apart from other Angelenos. His take on the customary Bud Powell template was engagingly relaxed and cheerful without sacrificing gravitas. Partial to the overtly melodic, he easily found safe haven with variety act entertainers in later years when jazz was upstaged by rock music. After a long hiatus, (almost twenty-five years), a Bill Evans-inspired

Freeman surfaced from time to time on recordings which are not without interest.

"A Clumsy Girl Named Grace" recalls Freeman's days with Chet Baker and Shelly Manne. The form is unusual: a twelve-bar blues head with a repeat, followed by an eight-bar bridge and a recap of the head. Freeman rarely used the blues as a forum for maudlin, sad-sack outpourings, as we shall see. The minor 2nd grind in the C chord at the very outset of the piece is impish, and the ensuing line makes few if any concessions to sobriety. Bars 5 and 6 demonstrate the good-natured qualities of tritones (augmented 4ths) when used in the right context. On beats 3 and 4 of bar 7, the repeated top notes over descending minor 10ths are typical of West Coast harmony's lighter moments. Bars 8–10 suggest that Grace has stumbled (in 4ths) on a pedal point. She regains her composure in the first and second endings.

Section B is a semitonal departure from the I–IV–V infrastructure of the blues. The chords alternate with single-note phrases in a call and response pattern—a familiar practice in jazz tradition. Section C recaps the head and ends with a playful solo break.

Freeman's sense of humor is not the monkey in a tuxedo kind; the sixteenth and dotted eighth note couplings in bars 35–37 are sly, not silly. The solo continues with a spate of double-timing sixteenth notes (bar 39), a device Freeman used more judiciously than some of his peers. From bar 41 through the end of the section (bar 46), the pianist shows his clear debt to Bud Powell, except for Freeman's fuller voicings and greater activity in the left hand.

The pentatonic scale makes its first full-blown appearance in bars 47–48, whereas previous encounters with it have only been fragmentary teasers. From bars 50–53, Freeman toys with a merry motif consisting of two eighth notes tied to a quarter note. Section E ends (bars 55–56) with a jittery string of seconds and thirds. Their lower notes begin on the 13th of the chords and descend by half steps to the 5th. The upper notes remain on the 7th.

In the solo's final moments, Freeman pays homage to Horace Silver, the secondary influence on his playing after Bud Powell. Silver's trademark pentatonics are appropriated for the dominant 7th chord (shown as 13 chords) sequences of the F section. The pentatonic scale was common coin among Silver's many disciples west of the Rockies. The bebop grandpop, as Silver is sometimes called, would probably wince, however, at the busy left hand work here. Freeman's strong left hand prompted the following entry in *Richard Cook's Jazz Encyclopedia*: "He [Freeman] often sounds like a particularly modernistic swing player."

Bar 66 heralds the G section with repeated eighth notes—pentatonics again. Over the dissonant sharp 9th chords in bars 69–70, another series of repeated eighth notes brings relative consonance to the texture. Freeman implements this sweet and sour combination until he reaches the key's subdominant chord at bar 71. Horace Silver's influence returns in the riffing, rocking thirds (bars 71–74), and the following V–IV–I sequence, where the ideas sound like retro boogie-woogie. Freeman's forays into Silver's style were based on a mutually sunny approach to playing, and rarely resorted to slavish imitation. The triplet coda makes a characteristicly high-spirited valedictory.

A Clumsy Girl Named Grace

Music by Gene Rizzo

LORRAINE GELLER

(1928–1958)

BIOGRAPHY

Born Lorraine Winifred Walsh in Portland, Oregon, Geller was introduced to jazz by her high school band director. The exposure sparked a sea change for a poetry smitten young girl whose promising sketches and paintings alluded to a career in the graphic arts. After an intense apprenticeship period spent in learning how to adapt her classical piano training to the styles of Art Tatum and Teddy Wilson, Lorraine boarded the band bus with Anna Mae Winburn's Sweethearts of Rhythm (1949). She relieved the tedium of constant bus travel for the next few years by sketching her bandmates.

Swing orchestras, even attractive all-girl swing orchestras, were dinosaurs in the music business by 1952 when the Sweethearts broke up in New York. Finding themselves stranded there, Lorraine and bassist Bonnie Wetzel formed a duo for gigs on 52nd Street. On "the street," the pianist rebooted a friendship with the alto saxophonist Herb Geller (a Californian, fresh from a stint with Claude Thornhill), whom she had met at a Los Angeles jam session in 1950. The two displaced West Coasters soon married and returned to Los Angeles.

Lorraine was one of the better equipped foot soldiers on the L.A. jazz scene, having added some potent bebop weaponry to her war chest in her New York days. She worked with Shorty Rogers, Maynard Ferguson, and Zoot Sims (1953–54), and co-led a fine quartet with her husband (1954–55). Her model accompaniment and high-grade bebop soloing made vital contributions to Red Mitchell's recording debut as a leader in 1957. Later in the same year, she gave birth to a daughter—a rigorous, heart weakening experience for a lifelong asthmatic. Back in harness prematurely, Lorraine shared stages with Kay Starr and Lenny Bruce. On the morning of October 11, 1958, after returning from an engagement with the Bill Holman/Mel Lewis quintet, she died of a heart attack. That Lorraine has been criminally neglected by jazz historians goes without saying, and too few of her recordings have been reissued to contest the outrage.

ANALYSIS: *Mynah Bird*

"Charlie Parker was pleased to see Lorraine in the audience for one of his dates on the Sunset Strip," Herb Geller recalled during a telephone interview. Apparently Parker was a more standards-centric player live than he was on recordings. Hampered that night by a local pianist's meager repertoire, he quickly pressed his former 52nd Street chum into service. "Lorraine was one of the few regionals at the time who could cover all of Bird's bases," Geller explained, "she knew a ton of songs and could really play. Everybody wanted to work with her."

"Mynah Bird" celebrates the solid musicianship that made Lorraine one of the leading pianists on the West Coast. Several dramatic close-voiced chords appear in the head, and most are cast in the lower half of the piano. Anchored in a sober tonality (C minor), they bookend the theme's lighter moments (bars 9–12 and 25–30). Here, the submediant chords A♭maj7 and A♭m6 serve as a pivot for the relative major key (E♭). On the third beat of bar 6, we meet an ambiguous voicing which the following A♭ melody note suggests is an Fm7(♭5) over a B♭ in the bass. A more explicit voicing of the chord helpfully surfaces in the same place during the improvised solo to bolster the suggestion. Lorraine sometimes escaped routine II–V moves in this way.

In the 1st and 3rd segments of "Mynah Bird's" A–B–A–C form, the right hand supplies not only the melody, but the lion's share of the accompaniment—a tricky specialty of this pianist in theme statements. How much this proclivity is owed to Lorraine's studies with L.A.'s resident jazz guru Sam Saxe is open to question. Saxe's many students included Hampton Hawes, who felt that he had "learned a lot" from his teacher. Lorraine's pursuit of musical self-discovery under Saxe's aegis may account for at least some of her stylistic earmarks.

The opening bars at letter C incorporate three bluesy statements of G♭, the flatted 5th of C minor. Bar 38 begins a stream of mostly eighth notes. Here, Lorraine is careful to keep the chromatic passing tones on the upbeats where their momentary dissonance with the chords are less jarring. This is the Charlie Parker tradition seen through the prison of Bud Powell. For contrast, an open-voiced D7 at bar 45 gives rise to a line with fewer passing tones.

Lorraine borrows some rocking octaves from Teddy Wilson in bars 49–52. Her left-hand accompaniment, a model of economy, begins with the interval of a 5th and expands chromatically to a minor 7th. The dramatic impact here is achieved without resorting to a clangorous "freak out." As usual, the pianist is rugged and forceful without sounding like she has a tire iron in each hand.

In bar 54, the ambiguous chord previously mentioned now becomes an emphatic Fm7(♭5) (labeled as A♭m6/B♭). The chord type's true progenitor in music history is not known, but Wagner used it so lavishly to open his opera *Tristan und Isolde*, that it is sometimes called the "Tristan Chord." Lorraine's voicing of it shares the piano's bass and tenor registers equally. Bars 55–61 are laced with bebop passagework. The first two beats of bar 62 repeat the blue note A before the chords in the following bars take us back to the head.

Lorraine was a continually evolving artist. "As young as she was, she was the best improviser in the band," ex-Sweethearts of Rhythm trumpeter Norma Carson remembers. "We didn't nickname her 'Jazz' for nothin'." A champion of Thelonious Monk before it became fashionable, Lorraine began to show some linkage with the music's newer ideas in the last of her 30 summers. Her death was tragically premature, even by jazz standards of longevity.

Mynah Bird

TRACK 9
Full Band

TRACK 10
Rhythm Track

Music by Gene Rizzo

VINCE GUARALDI
(1928–1976)

BIOGRAPHY

Thanks to his popular TV soundtracks for the Peanuts and Charlie Brown specials, Vince Guaraldi was unfairly granted less gravitas than a clown troupe tumbling out of a Volkswagen. The jazz police, in their infinite wisdom, had spoken.

Born in San Francisco, Guaraldi almost permanently damaged his right hand while apprenticing at the San Francisco Daily News in 1949. The accident green-lighted a switch to music full time. His swinging, appealing style kept him busy as a sideman with Woody Herman, Bill Harris, and Cal Tjader through the 1950s. He was also a Lighthouse All Star and occasionally collaborated with Brazilian guitarist Bola Sete on live dates and studio sessions.

Leading his own group in 1962, Guaraldi earned a GRAMMY® for his composition "Cast Your Fate to the Wind." His scores for Peanuts and Charlie Brown (1963–65) delighted an ever-widening fan base. Guaraldi was one of the few jazz artists to enjoy the 1960s in comparative comfort. Many of his peers were forced to choose between studio grunt work and/or accompanist gigs with lightweight songbirds.

Guaraldi's recorded *Grace Cathedral Concert* of 1965 begs comparison with Duke Ellington's *Sacred Concert* albums and the Masses of Mary Lou Williams. All three composers were really miniaturists too mired in simple binary and ternary song forms to effectively develop an extended framework. Ellington and Williams at least aimed for (and sometimes achieved) awe-inspiring moments, but Guaraldi complacently relied on charm and tunefulness. As poor record sales showed, the San Franciscan pianist's liturgical aspirations were not to be encouraged.

By the 1970s, jazz was released from its under-marketed doldrums by a new genre, fusion. Guaraldi had played some electric piano on Peanuts and Charlie Brown tracks, but was not interested. His popularity in decline, he died of a heart attack between sets at Butterfield's Bar in Menlo Park.

ANALYSIS:
The Lamplighter's Song

Trio playing can be a daunting challenge for a pianist. The de facto role of principal soloist calls for providing, at least, the illusion of infinite musical resources. That some West Coast pianists (Russ Freeman, Carl

Perkins, Lou Levy, Vic Feldman) left only slim discographies in the demanding format is less an indictment of their creative limitations, and more an exposé of unimaginative record producers. In any case, Vince Guaraldi's success as a trio leader was a no-brainer. The infectiously lyrical and rhythmic qualities that made his bones as a sideman never seemed to wear thin in a more central role.

"The Lamplighter's Song" recalls Guaraldi's thriving period as a front man and musical chronicler of the trials and tribulations of Charlie Brown. A halcyon mood is secured in the intro by two voices engaged in subtle modifications of an F chord. Guaraldi builds his theme at letter A, exclusively with chord tones. Bar 8 "answers" bar 6 by repeating the same melody notes an octave higher and enriching the harmony with a 9th. The peaceful harmonic rhythm is disturbed by three consecutive II–Vs in bars 9–11. Each V chord is introduced, however, by a II chord with a flatted 5th, as is this pianist's desire when circumstances allow for it. The theme comes to rest on the 9th of an Fmaj 9 in the first and second endings: the major 7th (E) appears low in the voicings to add intensity and slightly abrogate the finality of the chords.

Letter B begins as a paraphrase of the A section. Cast in D$\flat$, the key of the flatted submediant (a favorite modulation of Franz Schubert and other Romantics), the music deserts the paraphrasing to make a state-ment of its own. There are echoes of Bill Evans's explorations of tender jazz waltzes (e.g., "Waltz for Debby"). Given the tempo at hand, Guaraldi can hardly resist cribbing a little.

While letter C is a simple return to the music of letter A, at letter D, right-hand couplings of sixteenth notes with dotted eighths drive the line over the tonic and subdominant chords. The left hand, which relinquished the first beat of each bar until bar 36, now takes a more proactive role as Guaraldi enlivens a riff with his characteristic double grace note ornaments (bars 37–39). The remainder of the section navigates the II-Vs with the help of only a few passing tones. True to a pattern established at the outset, Guaraldi is an "inside" player, and very selective about his note choices outside of the harmony. He concludes "The Lamplighter's Song" on the Fmaj9 voicing that appeared in the first and second endings of the theme, but this time around, doubles the low major 7th to confirm the chord's finality.

Guaraldi is sometimes marketed as a forerunner of "smooth jazz," a label alien in his day, and one which he would no doubt have detested. Unsuspecting fans of the genre are likely to find more chord changes and genuine improvisation in his work than they bargained for. Perhaps Guaraldi's flair for melody hid his "rough jazz" essence all too well.

TRACK 11
Full Band

TRACK 12
Rhythm Track

The Lamplighter's Song

Music by Gene Rizzo

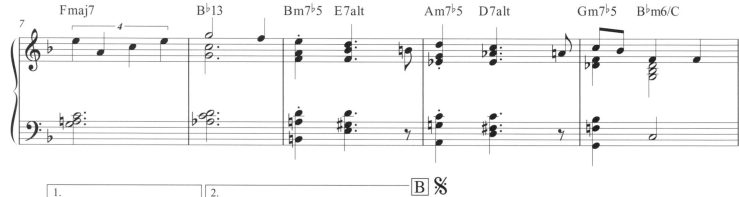

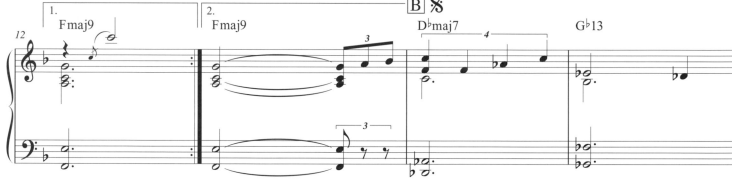

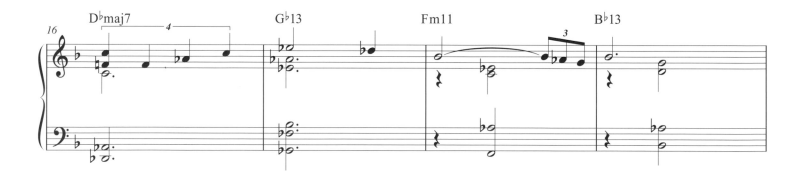

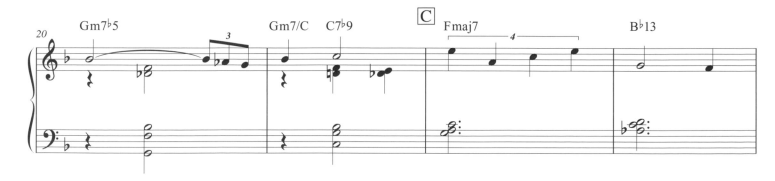

© David Redfern/Redferns Music Picture Library

HAMPTON HAWES
(1928–1977)

BIOGRAPHY

A minister's son, Hampton Hawes became a jazz musician without his father's endorsement. The outraged cleric continued to boycott his son's career, even at its very apex. Hawes's mother, a former professional pianist and organist, was more encouraging. With his mother's help, the budding sixteen-year old pianist managed to wrangle a paternal signature on a musician's union card application. The odyssey of an exceptionally creative but self-destructive artist had begun.

Hawes was born in Los Angeles, the youngest of seven children. Largely self-taught, his keen ears were tweaked by the pioneering style of Bud Powell. Hawes's early mastery of bebop took no prisoners at the piano in groups led by Wardell Gray, Sonny Criss, and Howard McGhee. Well-established by the late 1940s among the young guns of L.A.'s jazz haunts, he struck up a lasting friendship with Charlie Parker during one of the alto giant's trips to the Coast. He also began to explore the local drug culture.

After a dishonorable discharge from the army (1954), Hawes successfully resumed his career. His engagement at New York's Basin Street East in 1956 boasted no less than three *Downbeat* reviewers in attendance. This level of celebrity, and a full-fledged addiction to heroin, were bound to deadlock, and did so in 1958 when he was arrested for narcotics possession. When he was released by John F. Kennedy's Executive Pardon (1963), after serving five years in a Federal prison, Hawes had lost none of his crisp attack and propulsive beat.

Though plagued by a private life in tatters, he remained a musical standard-bearer throughout the 1960s. His conversion to electric keyboards in the 1970s compromised a style so personally ingrained "in the wood." The former hard bopper's fusion playing is not easily distinguished from many middle-of-the-road funksters.

Hawes has left a number of treasures, including three volumes titled *All Night Session!* (1956), a true milestone of recorded jazz piano, and an engrossing autobiography, *Raise Up Off Me*.

ANALYSIS: *One for Dashiell*

Horace Silver's subtle influence on Angelean piano players remains one of the best-kept secrets of West Coast jazz. Like Russ Freeman, Lorraine Geller, Pete

Jolly, André Previn, and others, Hawes was too personal a stylist to quote Silver chapter and verse. But elements of the Easterner's gritty conception surface often enough in his work to qualify as something more than affectionate nods to a peer. An uncommonly good blues player, Hawes's music is a synthesis of Silver's borrowings from Bud Powell and his own broad experience with Sanctified church music. When Les Koenig, the founder of Contemporary records, produced Hawes's superb *All Night Session!* in 1956, the pianist rendered generous samplings of his blues specialty.

Twelve-bar blues heads, not unlike "One for Dashiell," provided serviceable springboards on the date. A riffy trifle, its goal is simply to set tempo and mood. Hawes never attempted to create deathless masterpieces of composition. In the first ending he injects one of the only two grace notes in the entire example. He instinctively knew the device tended to sully his famously clean articulation and generally avoided it. One of the pianist's exhilarating solo breaks unfolds in the second ending. Spearheaded by the sequential replications of a four-note motif, it confirms his reputation as a soloist who hits the ground running.

Hawes rests at strategic places in the eighth-noted lines of letter B like a wind instrument player breathing between phrases. A practice that originated with Bud Powell's mimicry of Charlie Parker's alto style, the true intention of the pauses was often misread as flagging inspiration. (Many a low-tier bop pianist trafficked in non-stop blathering to avert the "stigma".) Hawes slips in a perky V of V sequence on the last half of bar 17. The rootless voicings of a B♭maj7 and a B♭6 in bar 21 present the remaining chordal essentials in fourths and fifths doubled at the octave.

The ideas in letter C, while Silver-plated, are otherwise Hawes's own: the sassy riff (bars 27–28), the oscillations between the 4th and flatted 5th of the scale vainly searching for a quarter tone on a fixed-pitch instrument (bars 31–32), the left hand defining chords in spare but effective two-part voicings (particularly bars 33–34), and the trip-hammer articulation of intricate bebop at all times.

Hawes's chorus at letter B is thoughtful, but not unhappy. (Russ Freeman, Hawes's closest Pacific Coast rival as a bad-to-the-bone blues player, might have approached it in a similar spirit. Unfortunately, neither artist has left us a truly reflective blues at ballad tempo. Such things were out of fashion at the time of the *All Night Session!*, and maddeningly continue to be.) No Hawes solo is complete without a snappy triplet that most pianists would corrupt by expanding it to a pair of eighth notes preceding a quarter note (the third beat of bar 33).

The music of letter E could effectively underscore a film scene in which a pole-dancer shocks a pious church deacon in a topless bar. Why the latter is there is best explained as creative license. The camera is on the woman during the riffs in bars 51–52, 55–56, 59–60, and cuts to tight close-ups of the deacon for the I–IV–I hymnodies in bars 53–54, 57–58. Hawes was equally adept at the sacred and the profane.

Oscar Peterson, one of Hawes's staunchest champions, referred to him as "my blues-playing buddy" in his autobiography, *A Jazz Odyssey*. Peterson saw "an extra glint in those bright eyes of his one day" and "knew that the drug dragon had sunk its fangs too deeply into my friend for me to be very hopeful." The dragon's prey eventually suffered a cerebral hemorrhage, lingered for two weeks in a coma, and died on May 22, 1977.

TRACK 13
Full Band

TRACK 14
Rhythm Track

One for Dashiell

Music by Gene Rizzo

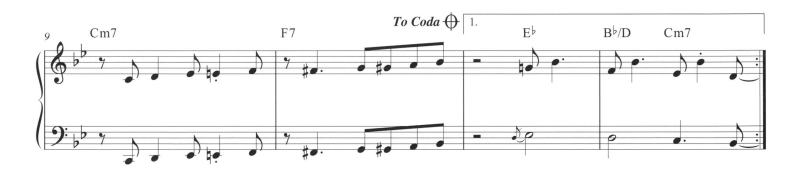

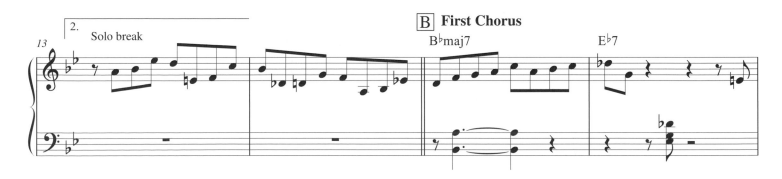

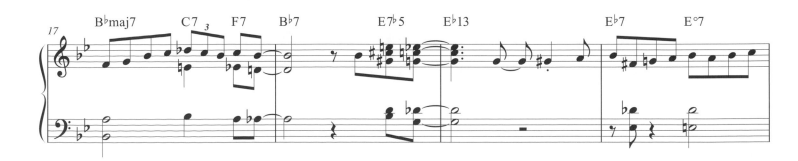

PETE JOLLY
(1932–2004)

BIOGRAPHY

In 1952, Pete Jolly (born Peter Ceragioli) took stock of the grim financial prospects for a professional musician in his native New Haven, Connecticut, and headed west. The then twenty-year-old pianist settled in Phoenix, Arizona, an easy commute to Southern California jazz clubs. Jolly's frequent jamming in such venues yielded gainful employment with Shorty Rogers and his Giants when Marty Paich vacated the piano chair to meet the overburdened demands of his arranging schedule. (Both pianists had more in common than their bebop-inflected styles; each had switched from accordion to piano at an early age.) In 1954, he recorded four swinging Giants tracks for RCA and signed an exclusive contract with the same label.

What seemed like a promising solo career lapsed into a profitable, but largely anonymous cycle of sideman stints. Jolly began to appear in a supporting role with practically every West Coast jazz leader, including Art Pepper, Terry Gibbs, and Lennie Niehaus, but seldom starred in his own projects. By the late 1950s, even remarkable solo features like "Over the Rainbow" on his former boss Shorty Roger's tribute album to Harold Arlen, failed to reach most record producers' hearing aids. In the 1960s and 70s, Jolly surrendered to the expediency of studio work. Except for occasional dates at Dante's in Hollywood, he worked in the shadow of composer/arrangers Neal Hefti, J.J. Johnson, Billy Byers, and Don Costa.

Emerging again as a jazz player in the 1980s and 90s, Jolly led an excellent trio (usually with Chuck Berghofer on bass, and Nick Martinis on drums) on live dates and recordings. The live occasions no doubt triggered requests for his best-known composition "Little Bird." In 1992, he added his romping style to nostalgic reunions of the Lighthouse All Stars. A number of crucial health issues took his life during a well-deserved retirement.

ANALYSIS: *Rose of the South*

Jolly was sometimes overqualified to function as a sideman, but the role of a trio leader fit him like a diver's wet suit. His playing in a trio setting showed exemplary restraint for an artist whose fiery imagination was often grounded in mid-flight by leaders hogging solo space. There is also something to be said for a pianist who can easily convene the same fine rhythm section for nearly two decades. Jolly's trio projects, however modest in number, were comparable in quality to those of Hampton Hawes and Phineas Newborn. He was, however, more willing than they to distance himself from an abundant technique whenever he perceived it to be a melodic liability.

"Rose of the South" has the kind of plus-size melody Jolly liked to play with his trio at up tempo. Rich in *appoggiaturas* (notes within a chord moving from dissonance to consonance by half or whole step), unhurried in harmonic rhythm, it alludes to the many operetta-like "bon-bons" in the group's repertoire. Most of the head lies above the treble staff, a range Jolly customarily used for bright, single-noted lines. The form is A–A–B–C. There is a bit of locked-hands style in bars 27–28, but the left-hand accompaniment is independent otherwise. Little has been done to disguise the schmaltzy origins of the melody; unabashed romanticism is not a contradiction in this pianist's swinging conception.

The solo segment opens with a pair of related two-bar phrases (bars 33–36). The second one is a terse summary of the first. Jolly approaches and leaves the F♯ appoggiatura in bar 38 by half-step. Taking a cue from Red Garland, one of Jolly's favorite pianists, bars 41–42 are lightly frosted with arpeggiated triads. (The cribbing of Garland's stabbing left hand style can hardly pass notice for those familiar with it.) Jolly's "voice" is personal, but his heroes, including Bud Powell and Horace Silver, are never far from his thoughts.

The phrases of letter E make an effective combined statement regardless of the incremental construction. The rests never threaten the line's driving momentum—if anything, they accentuate it. If the rests were replaced by eighth notes joining the phrases, the pianist's clever artifice would be reduced to a commonplace chain of licks. Jolly's ability to pull off such finger-friendly hat tricks at blistering up tempos explains why he doesn't always sound as technically brilliant as other members of the Coast's keyboard fraternity.

Bars 57–60 are tunefully executed with primary chord tones. The authority of the subdominant, which previously claimed all four beats of bar 58 and its antecedents in previous choruses, is challenged for the first time by the addition of a diminished 7th chord (in the left hand, on the "and" of beat 2, bar 58). The return of the home key chord a quarter note early (on beat 4 of bar 58) further questions that authority. Jolly transverses the V of V sequence in bars 61–62 with some well-placed passing tones in the line. He uses classic bebop turnbacks (III–♭III–II–V) in bars 63–64.

Jolly's left hand relinquishes its accompanimental role at bar 69. Acting as a kind of herald on the first beat of each bar until bar 74, it announces three right-hand phrase fragments before withdrawing from the forefront. In bar 76, the right hand assertively discharges a pair of octaves; only a slight adjustment is needed to convert the supporting left-hand chords from a 13th to an augmented 5th. Jolly's final phrases before taking the *dal segno* contain enough primary tones to identify their chordal sources. The ending comes courtesy of Bill Basie, who often lended a hand at such times.

For a glimpse of Jolly in action, watch the Academy Award®-winning film *I Want to Live* (1958). He appears in the opening nightclub scene, playing with Shelly Manne, Bud Shank, Frank Rossolino, and others behind a cloud of cigarette smoke.

Rose of the South

TRACK 15
Full Band

TRACK 16
Rhythm Track

Music by Gene Rizzo

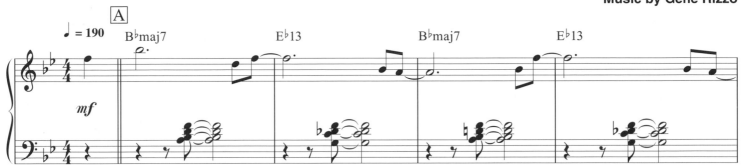

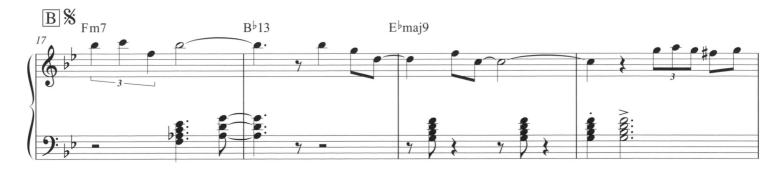

LOU LEVY
(1928–2001)

BIOGRAPHY

Chicago-born Lou Levy was road-tested in the bands of Georgie Auld, Boyd Raeburn, and Woody Herman before he entered his twenties. After a career change (the medical publishing business, from 1951–54), he returned to music as house pianist at Chicago's Blue Note. Well past the protean stage of developing a personal style by the mid 1950s when he made his home in southern California, Levy began working with the West Coast's usual suspects. He was Pete Jolly's replacement with Shorty Rogers's Giants, shone brightly as a Lighthouse All Star, and often appeared with Stan Getz during the tenor giant's L.A.-based days. Levy was already accumulating a vast discography. His recordings from this period with Getz, Conte Candoli, and Frank Rosalino are especially good.

When jazz was sucker-punched by rock in the 1960s, Levy paid the rent in the employ of pop singers Peggy Lee, Ella Fitzgerald, and Nancy Wilson. Adding to the most impressive Rolodex of vocal clients this side of Jimmy Rowles, Levy accompanied Lena Horne, Tony Bennett, and Frank Sinatra in the 1970s. He also played several of Sinatra's private New Year's parties. A popular course the pianist taught at the Dick Grove School of Music was discontinued because of commitments to several divas and divos.

Levy was still content to play a supporting role on most of his later recording session calls (e.g., with Supersax). He always acquitted himself well as an impeccable time-keeper in the rhythm section, and his vacuum cleaner ears were an asset to any soloist's trip to the mike. Levy's few solo albums for Verve in the mid-1990s echo the styles of Art Tatum and Bud Powell without surrendering a personal voice.

An attempt at drug rehabilitation—bankrolled by a surprising benefactor, Herb Alpert—failed to curb Levy's many years of heroin addiction in his last days. The pianist's death rocked the L.A. musical establishment, which held him in high regard.

ANALYSIS: *High Stakes*

The recorded collaborations between Levy and Stan Getz rival the best efforts of Dave Brubeck with Paul Desmond, Lorraine Geller with Herb Geller, and Russ Freeman with Chet Baker. Getz apparently realized the synergism and featured it often through the years. In 1996, five years after Getz's death, Levy appeared in the posthumous tribute, Three Getz Pianos, at the JVC festival in New York. Among the dynamic duo's many recordings together, *The Steamer* (1956), stands as one of their best. Each player's solo space on the session is inventively recycled in the other's, a pattern not unlike a theme and variations. The theme, however obliquely referenced, can always be traced to somewhere in the previous solo. Apart from his crafty exchanges with Getz, Levy also gives some object lessons in accompaniment.

"High Stakes" is suggested by repertoire culled from *The Steamer*. There is no head—the solo is an improvisation from the start. Levy uses the I chord's tonic five times before he ends the opening phrase on the bluesy subdominant in bar 3. (Interestingly, this a standard I–IV blues progression thus far, except for the premature placement of the subdominant.) A second lengthier phrase begins in bar 4 and extends to the first beat of bar 9. Levy is generally a longer line-spinner than others on the Coast. On balance, his style reflects the overtly pianistic tradition of Bud Powell, rather than the Horace Silver "hornistic" one. Extended phrases with no subdivisions continue in bars 9–12 and 13–16. A new line erupts in the last half of bar 16 and blithely carries on for the next four measures. Because of his sure-fingered articulation and tasteful note choices, Levy is in no danger of sounding reckless.

An eight-bar bridge unfolds at letter B. The line that begins in bar 16 is crowned with altered extensions in thirds (bar 18), and concludes with a little bebop epigram (bars 19–20). In bars 21–24, Levy opens up his left-hand harmony to support two more epigrams. Well-constructed, harmonically volatile bridges are holy writ to Levy. He rarely skates through them with stock licks—a remarkable history to which many musicians cannot lay claim.

For his third encounter with the I–IV progression (bars 25–28), Levy turns to pentatonics. The IV chord has by now lost the bluesy implications it had at the beginning of the solo. Levy is not a gutbucket pianist, per se, in the way that Hampton Hawes and Les McCann are. By bar 28, primary chord tones have eclipsed the pentatonics. As always with this pianist, the left hand tastefully supports the melodic activity, confirming his manifest expertise as an accompanist. In bar 32, an E♭7+ chord completes a dynamic cycle of turnbacks, and signals a gathering storm.

The dramatic outburst of chords voiced in fourths (bars 33–36) galvanizes the solo. For all of their upper-register clangor, the chords deliver a simple riff, based on the Mixolydian mode. Peace and calm are reclaimed in the chirpy single-note line sequel (bars 37–40). Modeled on big band chart, exchanges between a full-throated written ensemble and an improvising soloist, the contrasting procedure is unique to Levy on a last chorus such as this. In bars 41–48 the device is reprised.

Had the lines in letter E been blown through a tenor saxophone, they would easily have passed for vintage Stan Getz. Levy was not predisposed to many horn influences, but his *Steamer* partner was definitely one of them. Also, no disciple of Bud Powell has ever escaped a debt to Charlie Parker. After some exultant octave riffing, Levy suspends a II–V–I progression in bars 62–63 and goes for a tag. The II–V–I is carried through in the final bars, albeit, with some lush modifications.

High Stakes

TRACK 17
Full Band

TRACK 18
Rhythm Track

Music by Gene Rizzo

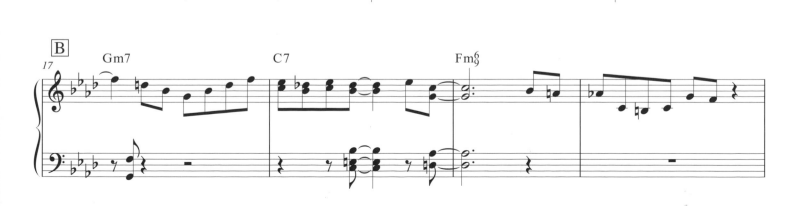

© David Redfern/Redferns Music Picture Library

LES McCANN
(1935–)

BIOGRAPHY

In 1958, the Hillcrest Club, a seedy Los Angeles watering hole, hosted Monday-night jam sessions under the leadership of Les McCann. A couple of hit records later, McCann's party-hearty piano style could be heard at more prestigious venues where appreciative crowds gathered at noise levels comparable to a pack of Hell's Angels roaring their Harleys through a small town. In the absence of newer hits over the years, the crowds fell away, swore their allegiance to other prophets, and reduced a once celebrated career to a footnote.

Leslie Coleman McCann was born in Lexington, Kentucky. His formative music studies were equally divided between piano and voice. In 1956, he sang on "The Ed Sullivan Show" after winning a Navy talent contest. A move to L.A. in the late 1950s provided a lively marketplace for his piano playing and occasional vocals. McCann worked briefly as Gene McDaniels's accompanist before signing with Pacific Jazz (1960), where he recorded a spate of popular albums rooted in the gospel-tinged, soul-jazz style. Spiraling record sales made him a star attraction on the jazz festival circuit. In 1969, his partnership with saxophonist Eddie Harris at the Montreux Jazz Festival produced the hit "Compared to What."

McCann's commercially risky ventures in the 1970s with Art Pepper, Coleman Hawkins, and Zoot Sims tanked, and a restless, hit-starved fan base began its exodus. By the 1980s, he was stressing his vocal side and often played synth on a series of failed attempts to capitalize on other singers' chartbusters. The jazz content in his work finally ceased to exist. A debilitating stroke ended his piano playing in the mid-1990s, but he was still bringing his pipes into a recording studio as recently as 2001. McCann is disparaged by jazz critics (when he is remembered at all), but his grooves were as infectious as anyone else's in the funk-addled 1960s.

ANALYSIS: *Sister B.*

Hampton Hawes once rejected a lucrative offer to record some of Les McCann's most popular material or, as Hawes dismissively put it, "things people liked." According to his autobiography, *Raise Up Off Me*, Hawes played through a batch of songs that were under consideration for the project and decided, "I can't do it, I can't go against what I feel."

Hawes's comments indicate the extent of McCann's celebrity in the mid-1960s, when his bluesy, backbeat-driven sessions for Pacific Jazz were all the rage on both coasts. As it happens, McCann was only warming up for his signature hit "Compared to What" at the end of the decade. His early recordings, however, already adopted a highly successful mode of expression based on the informal jam session atmosphere of his old Hillcrest Club gig, and an appealing, if occasionally raucous, gospel piano style.

"Sister B.," a pastiche of McCann's Pacific Jazz days, draws on the personal touches that he brought to the twelve-bar blues form at the time. The head's common use of F (the lowered seventh of the G major scale) identifies the Mixolydian mode and duly "sanctifies" the infrastructure. Single-note declarations are paired with chordal replies to evoke the timeless call and response pattern of gospel choirs. Clearly, this is not your father's West Coast Jazz! McCann's voicings of the three basic blues chords (I–IV–V) highlight their respective Mixolydian sevenths. He continues to exploit the mode by adding ♭III triads to the progressions in bars 1, 3, 5, 7 and 9 (the C6 chord in bar 9 is substituting for F, which would be the ♭III of the D7 chord that begins the bar). Inversions of triads, as we can see by their proliferation in the head, are very adaptable to this style.

McCann's left hand pokes at tritones throughout letter B. The spare but resonant interval that reduces the essential blues chords to couplings of thirds and sevenths is easily moved about at the appropriate times. Harmonic considerations aside, this section pits a Charleston rhythm in the left hand with a 12/8 feel

in the right. The melodic line offers many a blue note, but reaches for higher extensions only in bar 18 where we find two statements of the pitch A, the 13th of the prevailing C7 chord.

The solo takes a decidedly secular turn at letter C. McCann's minor-third tremolos in this section share a common bond with the early blues pianists of the Mississippi Delta who, unfettered by the constraints of classical training, combined awkward fingerings with unorthodox harmony to mimic train whistles and harmonicas. This is the juke joint side of McCann that repelled even a bedrock blues player like Hampton Hawes. The tremolos are particularly effective in bars 30, 31, 34 and 35, where high register placement maximizes their impact. The device is cheerfully rounded off by thirds and single notes. There are also new elements in the Charleston accompaniment: chord tonics and their corresponding fifths have been added within fractions of a beat at the bar lines.

Letter D is already kick-started in bar 38 where McCann begins a new accompaniment pattern. The pattern's destiny as a two-bar ostinato is soon made rainwater clear. It will join in a somewhat different take on the call and response exchanges first applied in the head. McCann has reassembled his gospel choir: the yin and yang factions of it overlap in this incarnation, but their cleavage remains distinct. Mixolydian sevenths appear in the many I–IV progressions. Conveniently, their semitonal distance from the third of the IV chords poses no voice-leading problems. After the recap of the head, McCann ends his coda with a triumphant amen cadence.

Sister B.

Music by Gene Rizzo

PHINEAS NEWBORN, JR.
(1931–1989)

BIOGRAPHY

The careers of virtuoso jazz pianists are rarely destined for a long shelf life. The impact of weapons-grade piano chops soon wanes and allegations of a shallow, dispassionate style takes its place. Even Art Tatum and Oscar Peterson have never completely eluded the curse. Few of the instrument's alpha technicians, however, have been kicked to the curb as quickly and unceremoniously as Phineas Newborn. Shortly after his much ballyhooed debut on the New York jazz scene in the last half of the 1950s, he divided the remaining years of his life nursing a fragile celebrity in Southern California and Memphis, Tennessee.

A native of Whiteville, Tennessee, Newborn underwent rigorous concert piano training there and studied several brass and reed instruments. After spells with his father's rhythm and blues group (late 1940s), Lionel Hampton (1950 and 1952), and the Army Band (1953–55), he returned to his hometown, content to stay local. In 1956, Count Basie and jazz entrepreneur John Hammond convinced Newborn to present his dazzling wares at New York's Basin Street East. The engagement created a sensation, and a painfully shy pianist was placed in the unenviable position of qualifying as Art Tatum's successor. But a flurry of recordings (Atlantic, RCA), a duo soundtrack with Charles Mingus for the film *Shadows* (1958), and two European tours (1958–59) were dismissed as "all sizzle, no steak."

Newborn moved to Southern California (early 1960s) where he failed to make nice with his critics after four albums on Contemporary. Compounding a career in decline, he suffered a hand injury and was twice committed to Camarillo State Hospital for nervous breakdowns. His star-crossed career fared no better when he returned to his home state in the 1970s; several of his fingers were broken during a vicious mugging in Memphis. Newborn was poised for a comeback by the 1980s, but his recording activities had ground to a halt. Dog-eared scores of Alexander Scriabin's fiendishly difficult piano sonatas were found on his music rack at the time of his passing.

ANALYSIS: *Redemption*

Newborn recorded his first attempts at restraining his formidable technique in Los Angeles. From the albums *A World of Piano* (1961) to *Harlem Blues* (1969), the last of his four dates as a Southern Californian, he traded superficial flash for imaginative harmony, more expressive ideas, and finely graded dynamics. For the most part, his command of the instrument no longer called undue attention to itself. (André Previn, another virtuoso pianist and a fellow Angeleno at the time, made similar stylistic adjustments, but for other reasons. Jazz playing was not his day job. He could afford to enjoy it as a hobby without taxing himself to the limit.) In retrospect this was, arguably, Newborn's most creative period. He had found a good balance between form and content, which he sabotaged in later years by oversimplification.

"Redemption" concentrates on Newborn's brightest moments as a West Coast jazz musician. The intro delays a V–I (the Cm7/F functions as a V chord) cadence until its sixth bar. Dispensing with the formality of a head statement, Newborn begins with immediate improvisation. He navigates the familiar first sixteen bars of rhythm changes with a riff (bars 9–12), a three-bar phrase whose final notes are echoed an octave higher (bars 13–16, making up a four-bar phrase, including the echo), and two contrasting phrases connected by ascending minor seconds (bars 17–24).

The bridge (letter B) features some of Newborn's fleet, but rhythmically four-square passagework—a favorite target of derision by his critics for sounding like hip Hanon exercises. Most of that element has now been purged and replaced by high-grade bebop ideas. The left hand support, while spare, is rhythmically and harmonically apropos. Note that only minimal alterations are required to define the rootless chord progressions in bars 26–30.

Newborn is prone to channel the intensity of Bud Powell at climactic points such as those in letter C. The fanfare-like riffs in bars 33–36 are an obvious homage to the seminal pianist, as well as the droning F in the accompaniment which handily relates to all the chords of the I–VI–II–V cycle. Bar 37 begins with a predominantly pentatonic line (the F♯ is the only anomaly), and the phrase it initiates ends with a bluesy plagal cadence (bar 40, where the Cm7 functions as a IV chord).

The second chorus at letter D opens with a continuous outpouring of parallel lines spaced two octaves apart. The procedure is so closely associated with Newborn that Oscar Peterson, who claims to have introduced it to jazz, ultimately limited himself to using it in small doses: "I didn't want any controversy over who started what." One of the few color resources available on what is basically a monochromatic instrument, the device can be a forbidding technical challenge at this tempo. Newborn executes it with his customary feathery touch and subtly shaded dynamics. He is on to Tatum's great secret of achieving maximum impact by playing at a volume level barely exceeding a mezzo forte.

For his second pass through the bridge's cycle of fifths at letter E, Newborn resumes the conventional hand disposition for rendering melody and accompaniment. The slackened harmonic rhythm reduces the chord changes from two to one per bar. For all of their confinement to the relatively narrow range of an octave, the chromatically enhanced lines from bars 57–60 are expressive and lyrical. They set the stage for two sequential phrases (bars 61–64), also infused with rich semitonal activity.

Letter F hosts the last eight bars of "Redemption's" A–A–B–A form and another demonstration of parallel octave bravura. Newborn's paraphrasing of Charlie Parker licks, rife with tangy passing tones, build toward a convincing climax. The home key's tonic is literally hammered out in the final bar.

Redemption

Music by Gene Rizzo

© Ray Avery/CTSIMAGES.COM

CARL PERKINS
(1928–1958)

BIOGRAPHY

One of the Midwest's finest jazz exports, Carl Perkins was born in Indianapolis, Indiana. Handicapped by polio as a child, he played the piano with his left forearm set almost parallel to the keyboard, skewing his hand at an awkward 45-degree angle. Although self-taught and unable to read music (even simple chord charts), the determined Hoosier mastered a number of difficult classical piano pieces guided by an infallible ear and instinctive musicianship.

In 1949 Perkins moved to Los Angeles where he joined the band of rhythm and blues legend Big Jay McNeeley. Shortly after recording with Illinois Jacquet (1951), he served in the armed forces during the Korean War. Discharged in November of 1952, he began drinking heavily. Bassist Leroy Vinnegar, master of the "big walk," and one of Perkins's closest friends, noted that "he had to go up to the front line and he saw a lot of stuff which affected him" (from a Leroy Vinnegar interview, *Cadence* magazine, March, 1989). The vagaries of a drinking problem were not reflected in Perkins's escalating career. By the mid-1950s, he had put in quality time with Oscar Moore, Frank Morgan, Dexter Gordon, Art Pepper, and the first edition of the Clifford Brown/Max Roach quintet before the group switched seaboards.

The best remembered of Perkins's associations was with the Curtis Counce Group (1956–58). Counce, a bassist with a plus-size sound, presided over the most groove-oriented quintet in L.A. at the time—a perfect showcase for Perkins's leanings toward the hard bop end of the jazz spectrum. Cast in the role of foot soldier as he had nearly always been, (*Introducing Carl Perkins*, 1956, is his only session recording as a leader), the pianist was nonetheless the keystone of the group and one of its most consistently forceful soloists.

There was precious little time left for Perkins after leaving Counce in January, 1958. Swept up in the powerful vortex of alcoholism, his life was drawing to a foreshortened close. On March 17, only weeks after recording with Art Pepper, he died in the L.A. County hospital of cirrhosis of the liver. His name is still mentioned in hushed, reverential tones by the Coast's old guard.

ANALYSIS: *Sassy's Blues*

Contrary to popular belief, hard bop was alive and well on the West Coast in the 1950s. Carl Perkins thrived in the company of the style's major practitioners—the first edition of the Max Roach/Clifford Brown Quintet and the Curtis Counce Group. In spite of Roach's superb drumming, the pianist found more suitable rhythm section teammates for his hair-trigger time and funky solo work when he joined Counce in 1956. Perkins on piano, Counce on bass, Frank Butler on drums, Harold Land on tenor sax, and Jack Sheldon on trumpet, demonstrated a remarkable synergy overall. Two years later the wheels fell off when Elmo Hope replaced Perkins. The group's four CDs on Contemporary, previous to the personnel change, are cherished by serious jazz collectors.

"Sassy's Blues" is an impression of Perkins's style with Counce. The ensemble intro finds him doubling the tenor sax part below the trumpet's top line, but Perkins has the twelve-bar head all to himself. In bars 6, 9, and 10, restless augmented chords resolve downward by a half step to relatively open voicings of the subdominant and tonic chords. Perkins observes the good rule of using them only on the weaker, less accented beats of 2 and 4. The low root in bar 13 would likely have been played by the pianist's elbow because of his crab-wise technique. The left sleeves of his suit jackets were usually threadbare from the procedure.

Much of letter B bears witness to the influence of Nat Cole. Cole's habit of slightly detaching his eighth notes as though he were tapping off ashes from a cigarette, and his octave-laden ideas, are wrought in deliberate emulation. It was Perkins's affinity for such things, no doubt, that resulted in many gigs with the ex-King Cole Trio guitarist, Oscar Moore. Perkins's *Pacific Jazz* LP (1957), with bassist Red Mitchell and guitarist Jim Hall (our one chance to hear the pianist in a drummerless King Cole Trio context), was foiled by overdubbing a drummer after the session.

The story at letter C is told in a more personal voice, although some ears might hear cribbings from Hampton Hawes. The raw materials used by two of L.A.'s most potent blues pianists are bound to intersect at times, but comparing Perkins to Hawes (a favorite polemic among jazz connoisseurs) does an injustice to both. Their styles are as dissimilar as they are similar. In any case, the ascending semitones framed by waggish octaves in bars 37–38 should not be misinterpreted as Hampton Hawes-Lite; Perkins is simply a jauntier player than his more sober-minded colleague.

In bar 40, Perkins has already introduced most of the riff, which will prevail until bar 47. It rides over 9th chords, the latter rising and falling by half step on equidistant octaves—a riff unto itself. The figure's pitches either have a Mixolydian or a higher extension relationship with the harmony depending on the chord of the moment. Perkins is disinclined to pursue the riff any further at bar 48, where he launches a bluesy idea in triplets, ending on a sharp 9th. The pianist highlights this line over the V–I progression in bar 50 with his characteristic exclamatory octaves. The interval is heard again in the coda's repeated final chord; its penetrating sound italicizes a 13th, the only doubled note in the voicing.

Sassy's Blues

TRACK 23
Full Band

TRACK 24
Rhythm Track

Music by Gene Rizzo

ANDRÉ PREVIN
(1921–)

BIOGRAPHY

André Previn (Andreas Ludwig Priwin) was born in Berlin, Germany. Cast out of the Berlin Royal Conservatory in 1938 because he was a Jew, he joined the student body of the Paris Conservatory. In 1939, the Previn family fled Nazi-besieged Europe and moved to Los Angeles where the budding piano virtuoso's uncle worked as a film cutter at MGM. At 16, Previn's keen study of the recordings of Art Tatum and Fats Waller led to his substituting for Jose Iturbi, MGM's concert pianist/actor, on a film track requiring a jazz solo that Iturbi couldn't play. The precocious youngster's composing and orchestrating skills, bolstered by studies with Mario Castelnuovo-Tedesco, were also called upon at MGM. He earned Academy Awards for scoring *Gigi* (1958), *Porgy and Bess* (1959), and *My Fair Lady* (1964).

A grueling studio-work schedule never threatened Previn's interest in jazz. Together with drummer Shelly Manne (a personal friend for many years) and bassist Leroy Vinnegar, he recorded *My Fair Lady*, one of the best-selling jazz LPs of all time. This was followed by stylishly hip renderings of the Broadway musicals *Pal Joey*, *Bells Are Ringing*, *Gigi*, and *West Side Story*.

Previn's playing is marked by technical brilliance, razor-clean articulation, and harmonic practices inspired by such twentieth-century symphonic composers as Maurice Ravel and Sergei Prokofiev. Also, the West Coast pianists Russ Freeman, Carl Perkins, and Pete Jolly did not escape Previn's attention during his Hollywood years; he has filtered something of their witty, swaggering essence through his own unique sensibilities. Previn's famous "Like Young," an infectiously funky little piece, demonstrates his remarkable affinity for the blues. For all of these diverse elements, his style is personal and immediately recognizable.

Previn left Hollywood in the mid-1960s ("I worked for years in glorious Technicolor® and glorious anonymity") to launch a successful career as a conductor/composer for the concert stage. Currently the musical director and principal conductor of the Oslo Philharmonic, Previn still continues his jazz activities whenever possible on recordings and in live appearances.

ANALYSIS: *Theme for Babs*

Ballad playing is a slippery slope for a jazz pianist. The core of the problem lies in sustaining interest at a slow tempo. Art Tatum heads a very short list of ballad masters who do not sound sleep-deprived, bored, or otherwise disengaged. André Previn has earned an honored place on an even shorter list of pianists who sidestepped the genre's pitfalls without resorting to Tatum's coldly impressive bravura. A none-too-shabby player at any tempo, Previn is particularly convincing and original on ballads.

"Theme for Babs" is a portrait of Previn's achingly tender balladeering. The intro suggests a breadth and scope greater than the sum of its parts. With careful pedaling, the Mixolydian inflections, bell tones, and moving inner voices, simulate an orchestra in miniature.

The opening strain of the A–B–A–C form enriches a simple diatonic melody by adding 9ths (bar 5), hairline scrapes of a minor second, and occasional octave doublings (bars 7 and 9). The absence of Previn's "legit" chops and firepower are clearly intentional. Our born-again jazzman, who once played in a shamelessly Tatumesque style (and was less clumsy at it than most), has found his own poetic voice.

As bridges go, the harmonic scheme of letter B is fairly conventional until bar 20, where a II–V takes leave of what had seemed to be an unavoidable I–VI–II–V progression. The dominance of the key of F♯ minor in bar 21 is as momentary as the reign of D♭ major in bar 23. Previn's melody reflects the A strain's periodic rests on first beats. An active alto voice (bars 22 and 24) gives the line's starchy half notes some momentum.

Previn begins to recap the primary strain at letter C, but veers off course in bar 31. He pivots there on a Ravel-like mediant and takes up with the submediant in the following bar. Ever the subtle harmonist, he delays the full disclosure of the dominant sevenths in bars 33 and 34 with suspended chord intercessors. Previn's ending is simple and straightforward; there are no showy cocktail piano misadventures. The high-register major 9ths (on loan from Prokofiev) before and over the fermata, make eerie final musings.

Theme for Babs

TRACK 25
Full Band

TRACK 26
Rhythm Track

Music by Gene Rizzo

© David Redfern/Redferns Music Picture Library

JIMMY ROWLES
(1918–1996)

BIOGRAPHY

A native of Spokane, Washington, Jimmy Rowles's passion for tennis as a child made him a bemused piano student at best, until he heard Teddy Wilson. Other epiphanies with Art Tatum, Fats Waller, and Earl Hines diverted his attention from racquets and backhand serves. By his late teens, the die was cast, and he pursued a music career full bore.

Rowles was already a Bob Crosby, Benny Goodman, and Woody Herman alumnus before he was drafted in 1943. After the war, he worked with Lester Young, Charlie Parker, Ben Webster ("my second father"), and Zoot Sims. The gigs were concentrated in and around Los Angeles, where he made his home. A series of engagements and recordings with Billie Holiday launched a brilliant, if low-profile career as an accompanist with practically every major singer in the business.

The pianist's versatility sparked a profitable career (and further anonymity) in Hollywood film studios. He played the boogie-woogie calliope part on Henry Mancini's "Baby Elephant Walk" for *Hatari!*, and appeared on other Mancini soundtracks throughout the 1950s and 60s. The Hollywood years also bore some peripheral fruit: anyone who has heard Rowles's croaky, but musician-like vocals, will not be surprised to know that he was Marilyn Monroe's singing coach for a picture. When the great synth invasion swept Hollywood, replacing live studio musicians, he folded up his tent and headed for New York.

Participating in the 1973 Newport Jazz Festival rescued Rowles from obscurity. He recorded often and well in New York. For the Columbia CD, *Stan Getz Presents Jimmy Rowles*, he wrote "The Peacocks," an enduring jazz standard. Rowles returned to California in the mid-1980s, but poor health gradually reduced his work schedule. Toward the end, he occasionally appeared with his daughter, Stacy, a gifted trumpet and flugelhorn player.

ANALYSIS: *Shadows*

After his Newport Jazz Festival debut, Rowles became the darling of cranky record producers on a mission to preserve the pre-Herbie Hancock traditions of jazz piano. How this questionable goal was to be reached defies all logic: Rowles was a pianist whose abstract style was often misspent on long forgotten songs few listeners knew well enough to appreciate in imaginative reconstructions. A West Coaster only in the geographical sense, Rowles's interaction with major Angeleno jazzmen after the late 1940s was limited to film studio dates. His playing, marked by a snarky attack, sudden outbursts of dense chords fairly splattered at forte levels, and a tendency to play behind the beat, is Rowles's own.

"Shadows" mines the riches of the pianist's late period. One hears the intro's treble chords in bars 2 and 4 as either D♭ triads with augmented 11ths, or altered V chords. The configuration sounds more like a V chord in the head at bar 7 because of the G in the bass, but there is no B natural in the voicing to confirm it. Rowles traffics in interesting variations of the supertonic: the descending chromatic thirds in bar 6 and the ascending chromatics of the bass voice in bars 10 and 18. The form is A–A–B–A abbreviated to 16 bars, a pedigree which held a special fascination for this pianist. Who else could coax such exquisite beauty from sentimental warhorses like Richard Whiting's "Honey" and/or "My Ideal"?

The concentration on the lower register in the first six bars of letter B is Ellingtonian. Duke was one of Rowles's favorite pianists. Although the lines explore a higher range from bar 27 until the end of the chorus, the accompaniment hews to the instrument's basement. Rowles's frequent use of low root-position chords—a stylistic trademark—made him something of a connoisseur of bass players. Charles Mingus joined the classic Red Norvo Trio on his recommendation, and it was no accident that Ray Brown, who always enjoyed second-guessing a good pianist's left hand, played on two excellent Concord recording sessions with Rowles. (*As Good As It Gets*, 1978, and *Tasty*, 1980).

Bars 37 and 38 sport octave shakes a la Teddy Wilson ("I'll never leave him entirely"). Perfect fifths beat out a boogie-woogie tattoo under triads and thirds in bars 41–43, a sampling of Rowles's wit and humor. There is a snippet from the "Minute Waltz" and a spate of richly voiced chords before the rollicking pianist takes the *dal segno*.

Rowles may not be for everyone. A jazz musician with a flair for the eccentric, who specializes in bossas, middle-ground tempos, and ballads without hot-dogging through the chord changes, limits his or her fan base. But ears tweaked by a genuine maverick's approach to the music are urged to give Rowles a listen.

Shadows

Music by Gene Rizzo

© Peter Symes/Redferns Music Picture Library

JESSICA WILLIAMS
(1948–)

BIOGRAPHY

Jessica Williams's playing remains a well-kept secret, in spite of a fulsome discography (over 60 LPs and CDs to date). Williams's aversion to travel is partly to blame for her hazy celebrity; a first-rate creative artist, touring up-close and personal with her trophy wife good looks, could easily extend her audience. A disinclination to micromanage the business aspects of her career, compounded by commitments to small indie labels, haven't helped either. But ultimately the problem lies with the jazz press. It has been derelict in its duty to marshal the troops on behalf of this *rara avis* among post-bop pianists.

Born in Baltimore, Maryland, Williams entered the Peabody Conservatory at the age of nine, leaving its hallowed halls at seventeen with a virtuoso technique. Her piano teacher, Richard Aitken, tailored her classical studies to compliment her obvious skill at improvisation. Williams added to that a thorough investigation of the jazz piano canon. In 1968, she moved to Philadelphia where she worked with Philly Joe Jones and Tyree Glenn, and played electric keyboards with local rock groups. A San Francisco resident since 1979, she gained some traction in the Bay area by signing on as house pianist at Keystone Korner. Appearances with the eleven-piece Liberation Orchestra followed.

Jessica Jennifer Williams, as she was known in the early 1980s, recorded for her own Quanto and Ear Art labels performing on synthesizer as well as bass and drums via over-dubbing. She has come upon a signature acoustic piano style since the mid-1980s while borrowing from the collective consciousness of nearly every major jazz pianist, living or dead. Her beautiful time allows for all manner of liberties with melody, harmony, and rhythm.

The recipient of two NEA grants, Williams is a follower of psychiatrist/philosopher William Reich, to whom she feels indebted for cultivating the best aspects of her work.

ANALYSIS:
Central Avenue Stomp

"Central Avenue Stomp" fantasizes how Williams might approach a makeover of "Jada." Letter A is the first of four sixteen-bar choruses, each in tribute to a stylistically different classic jazz pianist. The format is typical of Williams's performances of shopworn songs.

Guided by her model continuity, the individual playing styles are cogently staggered; the process never becomes predictable or formulaic.

The "Stomp" opens without a head statement. Its dissonant intervals over a conventional stride accompaniment bear the unmistakable signature of Thelonious Monk. Williams samples the master's beloved major 9ths (bars 2 and 3), sudden whole-tone scale outbursts (bar 10), and impish grace notes (bar 15). Monk's conception is second nature to Williams. She has captured its willy-nilly earmarks, comparable to the serpentine flight path of a deflated balloon, on many of her recordings.

Red Garland fans will recognize his familiar block-chord voicings at letter B (octaves sandwiching fifths in the right hand: the left hand filling out chord essentials in the tenor register). Williams, who was still a child when Garland recorded with West Coast alto saxophonist Art Pepper on the milestone session, *Art Pepper Meets The Rhythm Section* (1957), plays Garland's "bag" with an authority that belies her years. She interpolates his droll single-note line triplets (bars 25–28), and returns to block chording to conclude the chorus.

Bill Evans, the most influential pianist of his generation, is showcased next. Williams has wisely chosen the Evans of the late 1950s and 60s. His introspective later periods would compromise the "Stomp's" driving thrust. The lines swing without relying on a steady stream of eighth notes. Quarter-note triplets, generally missing from otherwise Evans-esque solos (rare cases of the falcon not hearing the falconer), are used to good effect in bars 37, 40 and 43. Perfect fifths (bars 40, 42, and 44) lend poignancy to the phrases.

Williams celebrates Erroll Garner at letter D, but also brings something of her own to the table. The guitar-like strumming in the left hand and pervasive exhilaration are Garner's, however, he would not have cast his ideas in near unflagging double time, or reached for the higher chord extensions in bars 53, 55, and 56. Ms. Williams always reserves her own stylistics in these jazz piano testimonials for the last chorus.

Central Avenue Stomp

Music by Gene Rizzo